Action Sports Library

BUNGEE JUMPING

Bob Italia

Published by Abdo & Daughters, 6535 Cecilia Circle, Edina, Minnesota 55439.

Library bound edition distributed by Rockbottom Books, Pentagon Tower, P.O. Box 36036, Minneapolis, Minnesota 55435.

Printed in the United States.

Library of Congress Card Cataloging-in-Publication Data

Italia, Robert, 1955-
      Bungee jumping / written by Bob Italia.
          p.   cm. -- (Action sports library)
      Summary: Introduces bungee jumping, a sport for daredevils based on an age-old ritual practiced by the residents of Pentecost Island in the South Pacific.
      ISBN 1-56239-230-1
      1. Bungee jumping – Juvenile literature. [1. Bungee jumping.]
I. Title.   II. Series: Italia, Robert, 1955-   Action sports library.
GV770.27.I85   1993
797.5 -- dc20   93-15331
                                        CIP
                                        AC

Cover Photos: Allsport
Inside Photos: Adventure Photo 9, 10, 12, 20, 25.
               Allsport 4, 6, 13,14, 15, 17, 19, 21, 23, 26, 28, 29, 30.
               SportsChrome 15.

Warning: The series *Action Sports Library* is intended as entertainment for children. These sporting activities should never be attempted without the proper conditioning, training, instruction, supervision, and equipment.

Edited by Rosemary Wallner

CONTENTS

The Ultimate Thrill 5

Bungee Beginnings 6

Modern Bungee Jumping 9

The Mechanics of Bungee Jumping 14

What's All the Screaming About? 18

What it Takes to be a Bungee Jumper 20

A Call for Safety 22

The Thrill of the Jump 27

Glossary 32

No sport on Earth gives a greater thrill
than bungee jumping.

BUNGEE JUMPING

The Ultimate Thrill

For sheer, hair-raising excitement, nothing beats bungee jumping. This strange sport offers everything that the best carnival rides provide: danger, suspense, terror, exhilaration—and spectacular views.

Bungee jumping was once known only to a handful of sky divers and mountain climbers in a few countries. Today, bungee madness has begun to sweep the globe. Throughout the world, people strap on bungee cords. They climb high platforms and leap head first into the air. The best bungee operators are establishing safety codes and equipment to keep the risk at a minimum.

Bungee jumping is for adults only. Those who have made the plunge say there is no sport on Earth that offers a greater thrill.

Bungee jumping began on Pentecost Island.

Bungee Beginnings

Bungee jumping is based on an age-old ritual. For hundreds of years, the Vanuatu (van-new-AH-too) land divers of Pentecost Island have practiced this sport. (Pentecost Island is off the northeast coast of Australia in the South Pacific.) How the sport got its unusual name, however, remains a mystery.

Every spring, villagers collect *liana* (vines). The vines are elastic and stretch easily. The amounts of rain and sun in the months before April must be just right for the vines to grow with the proper amount of elasticity. The villagers wind the vines together to make long cords.

Once the vines are ready, young men scale high wooden towers. They lash the vines around their ankles and jump into pits of softened earth. The villagers consider a successful leap a show of courage. It is also a sign of a plentiful yam harvest.

None of the Vanuatu knows when the practice began. One legend tells of a woman who ran away from her abusive husband. She hid atop a tree. Her husband spotted her and climbed up after her. When he had almost reached her, she jumped and dared him to follow. Enraged, her husband jumped after her.

But the woman tied a vine around her ankle. Just as she was about to hit the ground, the vine stopped her and pulled her up. Her husband was unaware of the trick. He hit the ground and died. Despite the legend, only young Vanuatu men are allowed to jump. Women must stay 60 feet from the wooden towers.

Twenty land divers jump each year. Each man prepares his own diving platform and selects his own vine. No one is allowed to help him. This gives the diver a sense of self-preservation and forces him to look after himself— an attitude that is much different than on today's modern bungee jumping platforms.

A diver constructs his jumping tower without any modern tools. He uses branches and trunks from saplings. Each tower must be built at the crest of a hill. The surrounding area must be flat for the traditional dancing that accompanies the ritual.

The dancing plays an important part in the diving ritual. "If a jumper is too scared to jump," said one native diver, "he asks other men to dance some more to help get his courage up. Then, just before the jump, the dancers make a loud whooping noise to get his adrenaline going."

The methods of measuring the towers and the elasticity of the vines are unscientific. But the injury rate among the land divers is low. In fact, only one death has occurred in modern times. That death happened in 1967 during a visit by the Queen of England. The jump was held out of season when the vine conditions were not right. When the diver jumped, his vine snapped. Even the land divers have their safety rules. When divers ignore safety rules, tragedy usually strikes.

Modern bungee jumping began in 1979.

Modern Bungee Jumping

Modern bungee jumping began in 1979 in England. Members of Oxford University's Dangerous Sports Club (DSC) saw a film about the land divers on Pentecost Island. They decided to jump, also.

The club members bought a long elastic cord used for holding down canopies on jet fighters. They fastened the cord to a mountaineering harness.

The first jumps were often off bridges.

On April Fool's Day, the club made a trip to the Clifton Suspension Bridge near Bristol in southern England. To avoid detection by police, the members rolled onto the bridge in wheelchairs. They hid their ropes beneath blankets. Once out on the bridge, members fastened the ropes to the bridge. Wearing top hats and tuxedoes, the jumpers plunged into the Avon Gorge.

"We were terribly disorganized," said one member. "As we dangled from the bridge, we thought, how do we get back up from here? But by then there were police all over the place."

Later, the members jumped from the Golden Gate Bridge in San Francisco. They also jumped off the 1,050-foot Royal Gorge Bridge in Colorado. "That was the best jump," a member recalled. "We reached 111 miles per hour."

After the DSC's exploits made the newspapers, bungee jumping gained popularity. It happened first in Australia and New Zealand, then in France, and finally in California.

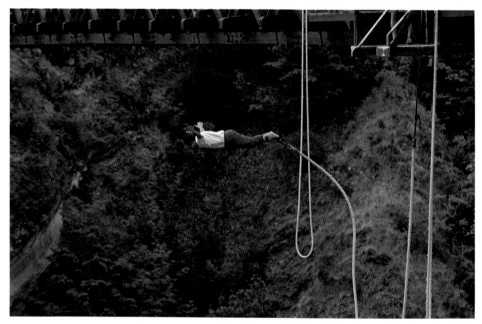

Bungee jumping began in America in 1987.

In 1987, two brothers, John and Peter Kockelman of Palo Alto, California, took a special interest in the sport. They began jumping from bridges over river gorges in the nearby Sierra Mountains. But bridge jumping is illegal throughout the country. The brothers jumped in the early morning hours or late at night to avoid arrest.

Finally, the brothers decided to start a bungee jumping business. They quit their engineering jobs in May 1988 and opened Bungee Adventures. Though it was unlicensed, the business attracted national attention. More and more people wanted to try the daredevil sport. After a slow start, bungee madness swept the country.

In 1990, the Kockelman brothers introduced hot-air balloons as jumping platforms. Every week, 100 jumpers from ages 12 to 72 paid Bungee Adventures $99 to leap from a tethered balloon 150 feet high.

Colorado was one of the first states to legalize bungee jumping. Jumpers visited Clear Creek County, where officials approved a 140-foot-high bungee-jumping tower on public land. "The best mountain climbers anywhere live here," said one bungee jumper. "Bungee jumping just fits in with the Colorado aura."

Hot-air balloons are used for jumping platforms.

The Mechanics of Bungee Jumping

One of the most important parts of bungee jumping is the cord. A bungee cord is made from hundreds of strands of elastic band. A nylon fabric is wrapped around the elastic bands. The rubber cord is fastened around a jumper's ankles or hooked to a body harness. The cord, which is as thick as your wrist, is long enough (usually 45 or more feet) to allow a few seconds of free-fall. Then the cord stretches and slows the force of the plunge.

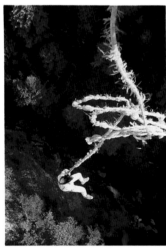

The cord is an important part of bungee jumping.

Jumpers leap headfirst from platforms. These platforms can be bridges, cranes, and hot-air balloons from 90 to 300 feet in the air. The jumper sometimes falls to within a few feet of the surface before rebounding into the air. Then the jumper bounces like a yo-yo before eventually stopping. Once the jumper has stopped bouncing, the jumper is unfasten from the cord before another jump can be made.

Jumping Platforms

Bridge

Crane

Balloon

In scientific terms, here's how a bungee cord stops a jumper's fall:

• Before you jump, you have lots of *potential* (stored) energy.

• When you leap off the platform and fall, your potential energy is converted to *kinetic* energy (the energy of motion).

• When the cord stretches, the energy of your fall is stored in the cord. This stored energy allows you to bounce back up in the air. Each bounce disperses the stored energy until there is none left. Then you come to a complete stop.

The most important element of bungee jumping is the *elasticity* (stretchiness) of the cord. The cord manufacturer and the jumper's weight determine the elasticity. The heavier you are, the more the cord stretches.

A jump master controls each jump. First, he or she weighs each bungee jumper. Then the jump master uses a mathematical equation and adjusts the cords properly. By doing this, a jump master ensures a safe and thrilling dive.

To be safer, some jumpers use two cords.

The equation has become so precise, a jump master can tailor-make each jump to heighten the thrills. "When we jump off bridges in California," said one jump master, "we ask the people if they want to just touch the water, dunk their heads in, or go in all the way. We can really get it that exact."

Some jumpers, who are a little less daring, use two cords. The jumper's weight is equally divided between each bungee cord, so the cord stretches half as far. The extra cord also provides another safety measure in the event that one cord should fail. Though the two-cord jump is shorter, it does not lessen the thrill.

What's All the Screaming About?

Another common element in bungee jumping is screaming. Bystanders hear screams from any bungee jumper—novice or veteran. So why do jumpers scream so loud when they are falling?

Scientists say that screaming is a common reaction to danger. It is a reaction that serves us well in threatening situations. Screaming gives our bodies extra oxygen. It provides energy we may need to run away or fight in life-threatening situations. This fight or flight response evolved to help us stay alive.

The fight or flight response begins when the brain senses stress or excitement. The brain instructs the body to pump out *hormones* like *adrenaline*. Hormones carry chemical signals that tell the heart and lungs to work harder. They also tell body cells to release more energy.

After the screaming is over and the danger has passed, elation may follow—often called a rush. That is because stress stimulates the body to create *endorphins* that are natural feel-good chemicals. This explains why people are so willing to throw themselves from airplanes and 150-foot platforms. Surviving the fall brings on a natural high.

The "rush" comes after the screaming is over.

What it Takes to be a Bungee Jumper

Adults don't need any special skills or physical conditioning to be a bungee jumper. But this sport is not recommended for the weakhearted. And it does take courage. Many jumpers say that the sport is scarier than skydiving. But the thrills outweigh the risks.

"With bungee jumping," said one jumper, "you have more time to think about what you're doing, so it's harder to jump. [When skydiving] from a plane, they hustle you out as soon as you reach the drop zone. The longer you wait, the harder it is."

"You get sweaty palms and cotton mouth," said another bungee jumper. "But the jump is one of the most elating feelings."

Bungee jumping takes much courage.

People bungee jump for the thrill.

So why do some people like to hurl themselves from 100-foot towers—and pay for it? Most agree the jump is for the thrill.

"I did it because when you're riding a roller coaster, I love the feeling when you go over the top and start down," said one jumper. "This was that feeling magnified a million times."

"It felt good to have done something that others wouldn't do," added another jumper. "There was a sense of accomplishment that went with it. It reinforced my view of myself as one who is willing to try new things."

"Jumping makes me appreciate the simpler things of life," said another jumper. "Like walking around a lake and appreciating what's there. But you won't understand until you do it."

A Call for Safety

Like skydiving, bungee jumping is not for everyone. There are risks involved. And there have been some deaths. Frayed cords, faulty platforms, and inexperienced operators usually cause the accidents.

Bungee jumpers should make sure local authorities have certified their bungee operator. Now that bungee jumping is a recognized sport, more and more states impose safety standards on the operators. Minnesota law requires inspection of bungee operators once a year by an insurance company. The operators must also carry insurance policies with a minimum of $1 million in liability coverage.

Not all bungee operators are safety conscious. And since the sport is growing so fast, there are not enough inspectors to go around. Some states, like Pennsylvania, have banned the sport. Others are considering the same action.

Bungee operators need to follow strict safety codes.

To be certain that a bungee operation is safe, Jim Hunter, president of Jumpmaster Inc. in Park City, Utah, suggests the following checklist:

• Ask if there is a "snatch-line" in the bungee cord. A snatch-line is a strong, thin cable that can support 10,000 pounds. If the bungee cord breaks, the snatch-line will prevent a jumper from falling.

• If there is a jump tower, look to see if a safety net or air bag is placed below. (Nets and air bags below cranes are useless because cranes can sway.)

• Ask the operators how many jumps have been made on the bungee cord. If they don't know, don't jump. If they do know, ask to see a log book. A log book records the number of jumps on each bungee cord.

• Ask the operators if they are conducting 100-jump inspections on each bungee cord. If not, don't jump.

• Ask the operators if they are using military specification cords. These are the strongest and safest kinds.

Bungee jumpers must listen carefully to the jump master.

The platform height is just as scary as the jump.

Each bungee cord should used only 200 times. To avoid frayed cords, the cords are stored out of the heat and away from harmful solvents. The best jump masters are thoroughly trained so that the calculations they must make are accurate. "If you use knowledge to reduce risk," said one operator, "you can make things safe."

All bungee jumpers must listen carefully to the instructions from the jump master. Failure to follow all jumping rules may lead to injury.

Most importantly, jumpers should follow the Number One safety rule: If you don't feel right about bungee jumping—don't do it!

The Thrill of the Jump

Many jumpers say that it is impossible to describe what it is like to bungee jump. But most jumps happen like this:

Your heart starts pounding the moment you decide to make the jump. Watching others jump before you doesn't help. And their screaming only makes you more anxious.

Your mouth grows dry when the jump master asks you to stand on the scale. Then your hands sweat as you sign the form as you realize you're really going to do it!

The climb to the platform is scary. You don't realize how high you are until you reach the top and can see all around you. The people below look like ants. The sight of them makes you dizzy, and you quickly look away.

Your heartbeat quickens as the jump master prepares you for the plunge. He or she wraps a towel around your ankles. Then the jump master wraps the bungee cord around the towel and fastens the cord with a clasp. Now you are ready for your jump.

Getting ready to jump.

Taking the plunge.

The jump master tells you to stand on the edge of the platform, which now feels small and shaky. You hop to the edge, your hands clasping the guard rails. You cannot look down. It's too scary. And now you find yourself leaning away from the edge.

For safety reasons, the jump master insists that you stand upright. Feeling short of breath and weak-kneed, you force yourself to stand straight. Then the jump master begins the slow countdown. You become petrified.

"Ten . . . nine . . . eight . . ."

You wonder why you're doing this . . .

You did it!

". . . seven . . . six . . . five . . ."

You wonder how you can get out of this . . .

". . .four . . . three . . . two . . ."

On the count of one you let out a howl and leap from the platform. Within moments, the ground rushes up toward you at 60 miles per hour. You scream all the way. Suddenly, the cord pulls taut and grabs your ankles. It pulls you up a second before you would have hit the ground and flips you around. Now you are headed three-quarters of the way up to the platform.

Suddenly, your second plunge begins. But this time it is a little less scary. You bounce like a yo-yo five or six times, your screams slowly turning into shouts of joy. As the bouncing slowly diminishes, you thrust your fist triumphantly into the air while a warm wave of relief washes over you. You did it. You are safe. You're a certified bungee jumper. You've done something few people have done before. And you can't wait for your next jump.

For more information about bungee jumping or jump locations in your area, write to:

Jumpmaster Inc.
P.O. Box 1644
Park City, Utah 84060

GLOSSARY

Adrenaline—a hormone secreted by the adrenal gland.

Bungee—an elastic cord used in platform jumping.

Elasticity—the condition or property of being flexible.

Endorphin—chemical painkiller that the human body produces.

Fight or flight response—your brain's response to a stressful situation. Your brain tells your body to either face the situation (fight) or get away (flight).

Free fall—the unrestrained movement of a body through air.

Hormone—a substance made in the body that helps it grow or stay healthy.

Jump master—the person who weighs each bungee jumper before making careful mathematical calculations to ensure a safe dive.

Kinetic energy—energy associated with motion.

Land divers—the name for young native men on Pentecost Island who jump from diving towers with a vine attached to their ankles.

Log book—a book that records the number of jumps on a bungee cord.

Military specification cord—the strongest and safest bungee cords.

Platform—the area from which a bungee jump is made. The platform can be a hot air balloon, crane, or bridge.

Potential energy—the stored energy of a particle or particles.

Rush—a sudden feeling of intense pleasure.

Snatch-cord—a thin steel safety line in a bunge cord.

Vanuatu—Melanesian inhabitants of Pentecost Island in the South Pacific.